G000291695

ISBN 0-9551005-0 X
Printed and bound in China. Phoenix Offset/The Hanway Press Ltd.
Published by: GIBSONS INTERNATIONAL LTD.
Project Consultant: David Buirski
Design Concept: The Quisk Consultancy

“There is no substitute for...”

Foreword by H R H The Princess Royal

Richard Proctor

In memory of Peter Valpy

Contents

Painters' Hall, 1992

BUCKINGHAM PALACE

There is little doubt that wool is virtually woven into the fabric of this country and its history and language appears to owe much to the fibre. The Livery Company, which once controlled its development and business in London, dates back to the 12th Century although its purpose in modern times has changed direction towards education and charitable works.

It was a privilege and honour to be both the first Lady Liveryman and Master of the Worshipful Company of Woolmen in 1994. I was delighted, therefore, when Richard Proctor, who was Master only a few years before me, decided to produce this book.

It can be construed as being educational in terms of its characters; it is certainly entertaining with its focus on a delightfully quirky but memorable part of wool's more recent history. The thinking and interpretation that lie behind the phrase "There is no substitute for Wool" may have been enjoyed far beyond these shores. I trust that this work rekindles fond memories for many and inspires those new to the subject to be just as creative in expression.

Anne

H R H The Princess Royal

Preface

In the brief period when Confucius held power in his home kingdom a citizen's dress was strictly controlled under threat of the death penalty. Later King Charles II made a wool shroud compulsory for those unwise enough to die. Nowadays wool producers must rely on an advertising campaign to increase sales. Nothing could be more charming than the solution of the 1950s when professional writers and gifted amateurs made up the verses in this book and the results, illustrated by famous cartoonists, appeared on the London Underground. Over the years many of the rhymes had been lost but, such was the devotion of the 1950s traveller to learning them by heart, most have been found again.

This is a book not only of humour but also of Western history as it was taught in the 1950s. The young today know every character on television: it is time to make sure they know this cast of characters so familiar to previous generations but often unknown to our children. And what a fascinating cast it is. Greeks and Romans, of course, but only Jonah from the Bible. There are two English kings but King Henry VIII is only mentioned for his wives; happily there are few real villains and even Judge Jeffreys would have put his victims on probation if he had been wearing wool instead of hot ermine.

Starting in ancient Greece and finishing with the first satellite all were designed to amuse Londoners. Let us hope that soon we see these posters back in our Underground carriages for every Londoner and visitor to read as they travel around the city.

I am not the author of this book only the compiler. It has been an interesting quest searching for these rhymes and I wish to thank all the contributors. Perhaps as you read this you may know of another rhyme not recorded here and if so we may yet have a second collection.

Richard Proctor
February 2005

The early ape-men (Pliocene)

Were men of squat and crouching mien.

And yet... what fascinating brutes

They might have looked in woollen suits!

For wool can flatter, wool can mould,

It dignifies with every fold.

This truth all tailors learn at school:

There is no substitute for Wool.

O foolish, frantic men of Greece,
To seek so long the golden fleece,
To comb all corners of the earth
For something of fictitious worth.
If only Jason had been told
The fleece that comforts is not gold!
But now the whole world knows the rule
There is no substitute for Wool.

Said Jupiter: "This peak is cold.

More nectar, please! I'm growing old.

What very foolish gods are we

To shiver here eternally

In fleecy clouds – while man below

Wears fleecy wool. Come on, let's go!"

The gods were wise to learn the rule:

There is no substitute for Wool.

Fair Helen was the Trojans' pin-up,
Her beauty kept the nation's chin up.
They say she was the only Spartan
Whose nose in winter wasn't tartan.
With fleecy wool she wove her wraps
Which kept her warm, and pleased the chaps.
She knew the olden, golden rule:
There is no substitute for Wool!

Fair Venus surfaced from the spray,

And not much work was done that day.

The elders came. They turned bright pink.

They coughed. They said: "We really think

Some well-placed wool would do no harm.

Indeed, it might enhance your charm.

Besides, you'll find the nights are cool.

There is no substitute for Wool."

When Jonah, deep inside the whale,
Seemed cheerful, hearty, even hale,
The whale said, visibly annoyed.
"But aren't you cold in that damp void?"
Quoth Jonah, with a careless shrug,
"My woolly gown keeps me quite snug."
The whale impressed, told all his school:
"There is no substitute for Wool!"

King Midas turned his goods to gold

By touching them (or so we're told).

The shimmer of his royal shirt

Bedazzled… but the garment hurt!

The royal socks were just as rigid,

And quite abominably frigid.

The King forgot the Golden Rule:

There is no substitute for Wool.

When Socrates, that learned Greek,
In ancient Athens used to speak
Midst Summer sun and Winter snows
When all but he just boiled or froze,
The rules of logic, laws of thought
Were two things that he always taught.
And added next the golden rule –
There is no substitute for Wool.

Pythagoras by stretching string
Extended maths like anything.
One day he tried some woollen strands,
And stretched them gently in his hands,
'What perfect elasticity!
It's just the very thing,' said he,
'To hold the shape of coats and wraps.
I think I'm on to something, chaps.
Let's teach this theorem at school:
There is no substitute for Wool.'

"Quo vadis?" cried the palace guard.
"Upstairs," yelled Nero, running hard.
"My wardrobe must be saved tonight,
Before the looters heave in sight.
The blaze is cosy now," said Nero,
"But mercury returns to zero
And when the nights grow long and cool
There is no substitute for Wool!"

Cried Cleopatra, curled up snug
Within a fleecy royal rug:
"I'll cheat the hosts of Ptolemy!
They can't keep me from Julius C.!"
"Good show!" said Cæsar, with a grin,
"I, too, like wool to travel in.
My edict runs where'er I rule:
There is <u>no</u> substitute for Wool."

Ancient Britons, blue with woad
Mostly had a frightful "coad"
Hengist and Horsa, when they raided
Clad in wool were doubtless aided
In winning those Anglo-Saxon scuffles
By being free from sniffs and snuffles
Proving the olden, golden rule
There is no substitute for Wool.

The robbers pounced on Santa's sledge.
Their teeth were very much on edge.
When Santa saw their ragged shifts
He took a bale marked 'Woollen Gifts'
And gave each knave the wherewithal
To shield his hide against the squall.
How snug each thug! They blushed with shame
And vowed they'd quit the hold-up game.
Thus wool produced (and always will)
Not only comfort but goodwill.
The message rings from Yule to Yule:
There is no substitute for Wool.

Quoth Wenceslas to aged peasant

"The night grows more and more unpleasant

I beg you, share my rich apparel

Accept it please, don't spoil the carol."

So king and peasant onward hied

With wool and friendship fortified

Proving the olden, golden rule

There is no substitute for Wool.

King Arthur's Knights sat sullen eyed.

"What ails thee all?" the Monarch cried.

Said one, "It's this round table, sire,

The lads out here can't feel the fire."

Quoth Guinivere, "Poor faithful knights.

I'll knit them all a pair of tights."

Morale was saved, which proves the rule,

There is no substitute for Wool.

Lady Godiva, so they say
Had longer hair than Danny Kaye.
It fell about her person fair
Concealing dainty underwear.
In winter warm, in summer cool
There is no substitute for Wool.

Macbeth surveyed the witches' pot
(Toad, entrails, bat, newt, frog - the lot!)
"Ahem," he coughed, apologetic,
"Tell me, is this a new synthetic?"
"Too right," said Meg, "and if it jells
It should weave other things than spells:
Highlanders' underwear, if worn - ?"
Mac winked at her, then said with scorn:
"Forbye we don't, forbye we do -
But 'gin we did, 't would aye be woo'"
(There is no substitute for Wool.)

An arrow pinned the sheriff's wig
Against the wall; he danced a jig,
"What gives this Robin Hood his nerve,
His vim, his valour and his verve?"
"We do not know," they cried, "unless
It is his all-wool battledress."
"In winter warm, in summer cool,
There is no substitute for Wool!"

King John in one fell splash (or splosh)
Lost bag and baggage in the Wash.
His courtiers wept as all went down –
The orb, the sceptre and the crown.
"Mere gems!" cried John. "A fig for those!
But oh, my vests, pants, shirts and hose!
If they are gone, I cannot rule.
There is no substitute for Wool."

As William Tell reached for his quiver
He saw his son begin to shiver
"Art frightened, lad, to face the arrow?"
"No dad, just frozen to the marrow."
They fixed him up with scarf and sweater
Then Will took aim again. "That's better
Lad," said he, then whang he shot.
The apple fell, the boy did not.
Proving again the golden rule
There is no substitute for Wool.

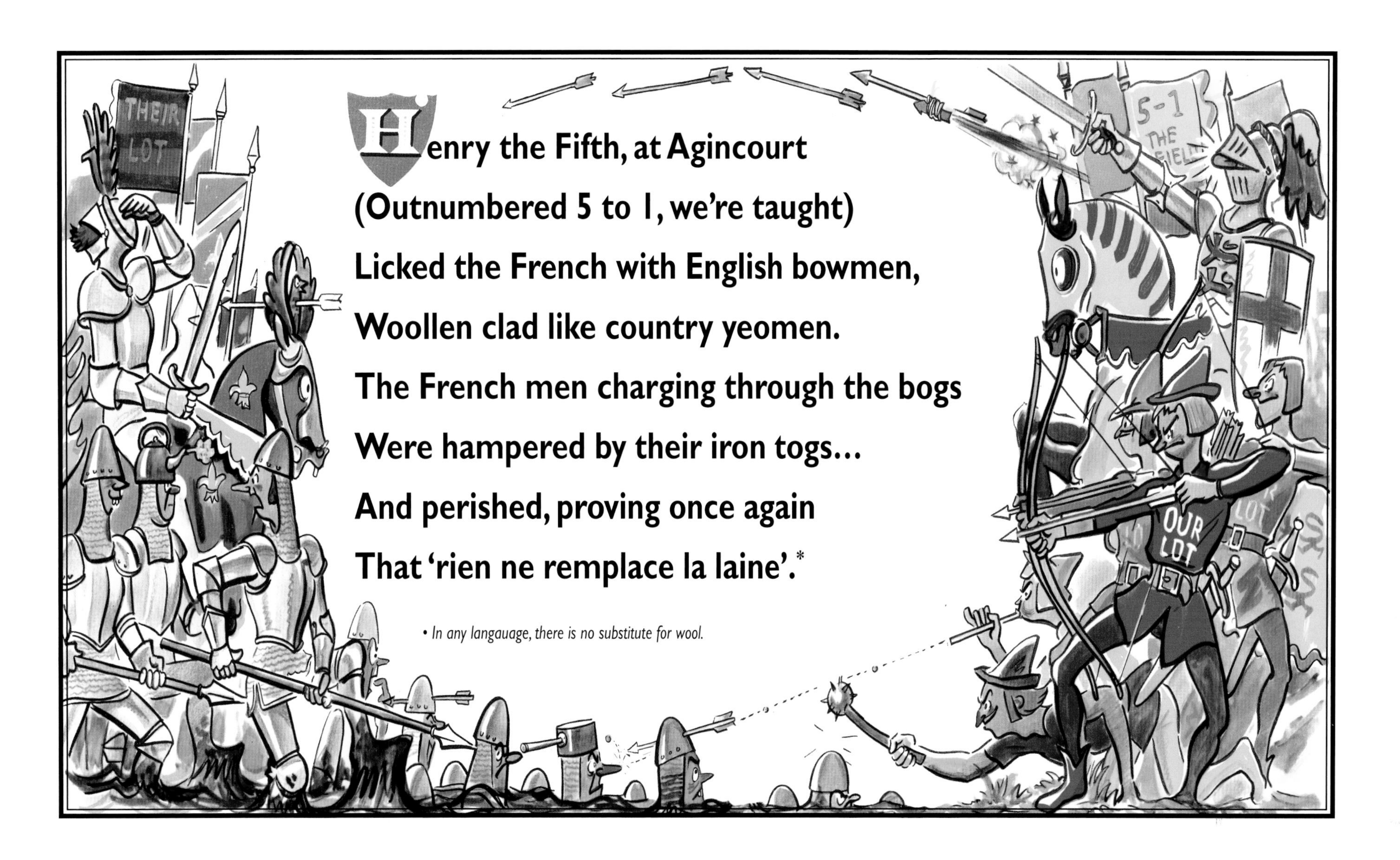

Henry the Fifth, at Agincourt
(Outnumbered 5 to 1, we're taught)
Licked the French with English bowmen,
Woollen clad like country yeomen.
The French men charging through the bogs
Were hampered by their iron togs...
And perished, proving once again
That 'rien ne remplace la laine'.*

• In any langauage, there is no substitute for wool.

Poor Gutenberg's first printing press
Was not a runaway success.
In vain he begged the local hacks
To churn him out some paper-backs.
The State, which scoffed at talk of grants,
Said, 'Use your press for creasing pants.'
Alas, the mingling of these arts
Stirred anger in his clients' hearts.
The printer, sore at their attacks,
Exclaimed, 'Can no one turn out slacks
With creases durably implanted?'
His wish, of course, has now been granted.
In this respect, wool scoops the pool.
There is no substitute for Wool.

King Philip, looking for a Queen,
Refused to take a bride unseen.
Said he: "I'll send some artist fella
To paint the lady Isabella."
Van Eyck was hired. With great success
He caught the magic of her dress
(Pure wool, of course), in oils enriched
The Spanish King was quite bewitched
He sent his equerry to get her
And rubbed his hands... and then he met her...
Which serves to emphasise one thing
That wool is highly flattering.
In Spain they say - 'Entendes Usted?'
There is no substitute for Worsted!

Columbus had a surly crew.
Each day more menacing they grew.
Yet spick and span and calm he stood
And told them whoppers for their good,
And tricked them with his Cheerful Chart.
Columbus was a man apart.
What kept him hale and confident
From continent to continent?
What nourished his immense resource?
Columbus dressed in wool, of course.
Explorers all observe his rule:
There is no substitute for Wool.

Of Leonardo let us sing -
The man who thought of everything,
Of guns and gears and gyroscopes…
What joy he had with wheels and ropes!
He brewed up dainty trinkets while
He painted Gioconda's smile.
In every art he had a hand,
His workshop was a wonderland,
And yet da Vinci lost no sleep
Attempting to invent a sheep.
He said, 'My friends, I'm no one's fool,
There is no substitute for Wool.'

Before Queen Anne Boleyn was sacked
She'd got her suitcase ready packed,
And labelled it, in letters large,
"The Bloody Tower, per Royal Barge".
Her friends all praised her savoir-faire,
Until they missed their underwear
For Anne, you see, was no one's fool,
There is no substitute for Wool!

When Anne of Cleves wed Henry Eight.

They sat up playing cards quite late.

The aces, held 'neath woollen sleeves

Were mostly led by Anne of Cleves,

For Anne, though somewhat plain, 'tis said,

Was smart enough to keep her head.

She knew the olden, golden rule,

There is <u>no</u> substitute for Wool.

"What weather," shivered Master Will,

"Ye ink is frozen in my quill.

I'm sure I'm getting 'sniff'atchoo'

...a dose of 16th Century flu."

Anne Hathaway produced a sweater,

"Ah! Wool," said Will, "My word that's better,

By keeping warm, I'll play it cool

There is no substitute for Wool."

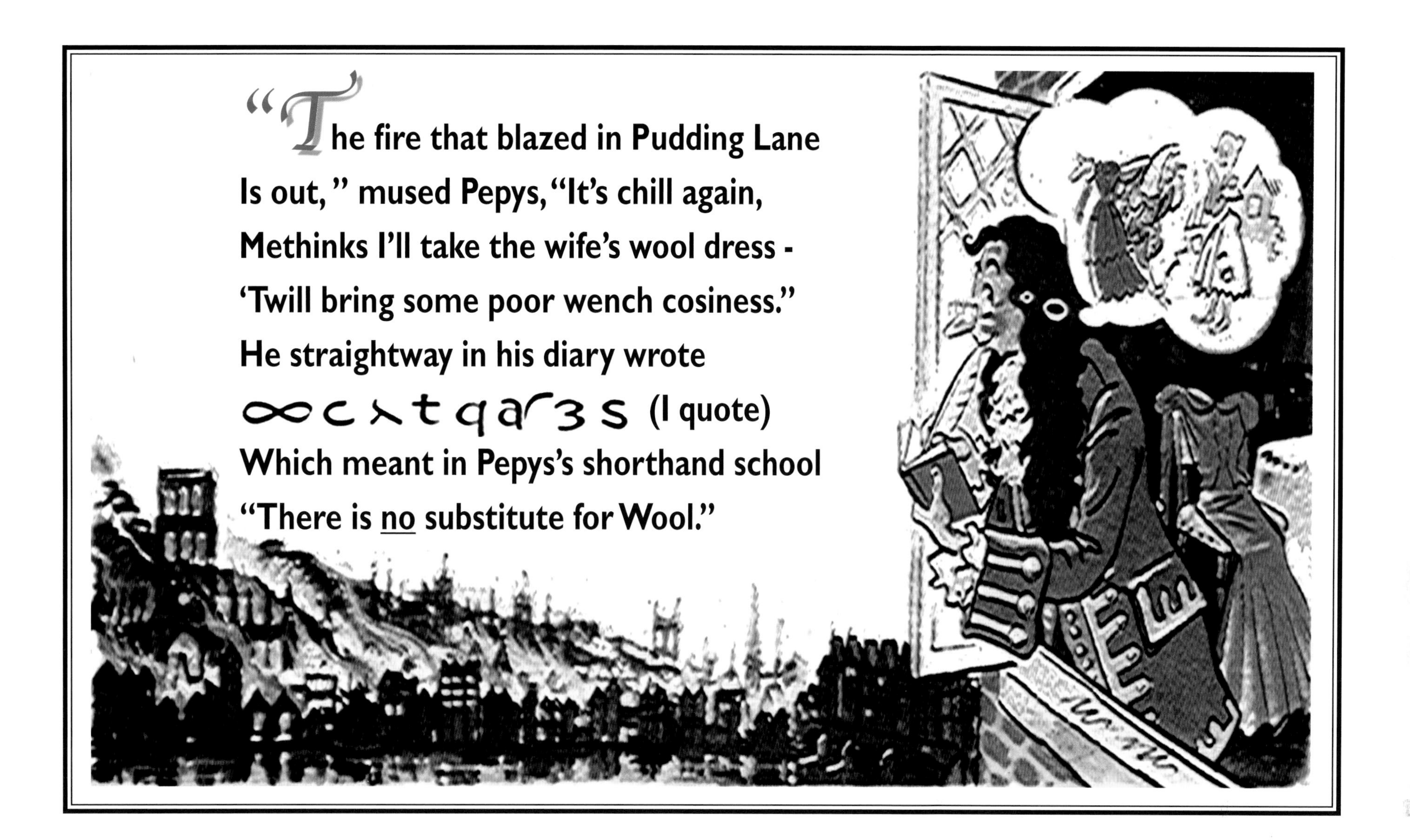

"The fire that blazed in Pudding Lane
Is out," mused Pepys, "It's chill again,
Methinks I'll take the wife's wool dress -
'Twill bring some poor wench cosiness."
He straightway in his diary wrote
(I quote)
Which meant in Pepys's shorthand school
"There is no substitute for Wool."

An electrician in a spin
Was dear old Franklin (Benjamin).
By dint of rubbing wool on glass
He hoped that splendid sparks would pass.
But wool is very little use
(He found) for generating juice.
Another thing: it won't attract
Soot, grime and grit. Which simple fact
Endears it to us. Mark this rule:
There is no substitute for Wool.

Judge Jeffreys felt extremely hot
Beneath his ermine. "Hang the lot,"
He cried - although his inclination
Had been to place them on probation.
If only he had known the balm
Of wool for comfort and for calm
Then mercy might have been the rule
There is no substitute for Wool.

When Louis Quinze of wayward ways

Held forth at midnight in the maze

Du Barry bored to suffocation

At least maintained her circulation.

Though nightly trapped in grove and grotto

She caught no chill – she had a motto,

One simple faith, one working rule -

There is no substitute for Wool!

"Our lexicon is finished now,"

Said Dr. Johnson, "but I vow

This entry **WOOL** is not our best.

'The hair of sheep' – how ill-expressed

For wool's the magic stuff of life,

It warms our bed, it decks our wife.

Be pleased to add, and under-rule:

There is NO substitute for Wool."

"Avast you scum!" cried Captain Bligh
(Three months adrift), "the shore is nigh!"
He siezed his log. "We owe salvation
To pluck - to faultless navigation -
To discipline - to lack of gin -
To wearing wool against the skin;
This last, a most essential rule:
There is no substitute for Wool!"

When Casanova went to Town

He always took his dressing gown,

His bed-socks and his knitted gloves,

Which mystified his lady-loves.

One gentle temptress asked him why,

Quoth he with an experienced sigh,

"Madam, I used to catch all kinds

of chills on those Venetian blinds,

So learned this lesson in Love's school,

There is no substitute for Wool."

Arriving for her pas-de-deux
This ballerina caused a stir,
For underneath a froth of white
A pair of stockings came in sight.
When challenged to explain her act
She said, 'It's an undoubted fact
These ballet tights are tutu cool –
There is no substitute for Wool.'

Lord Nelson was an admiral bold
Who beat the storms, the French, the cold
Because in fleecy wool he clad
Each jolly pig-tailed sailor lad
And if one tar so much as coughed
He had this signal run aloft
"Remember men, the Navy's rule
There is no substitute for Wool."

When Brummell Beau, the swell of swells,
Electrified the Brighton Belles,
The prince would hover in the offing,
Killing romance with fits of coughing.
"Another cold, Sire? Listen, do:
To be well dressed, be wool dressed too.
In elegance it is the rule:
There is no substitute for Wool!"

'The Rocket' thundered up the track
With fireworks streaming from its stack.
The public took it somewhat hard -
How tiresome to be chilled AND charred!
But Stephenson was on the ball;
He issued woollen rugs to all.
'They're proof against both wind and flame,'
He said. More honour to his name!
The travel-wise endorse this rule:
There is no substitute for Wool.

Yon canny Highland crofters keep
A breed of crease-resistant sheep.
They weave wee woollen skirts and slacks,
And sell them to the Sassenachs.
Wool keeps its shape, it's bound to please-
You've nae seen sheep with baggy knees!
At birth bairns learn the Highland rule:
There's still no substitute for Wool.

When Rip Van Winkle stayed in bed

His friends got anxious: 'Is he dead?'

If not, could he withstand the chills

Which blew around the Catskill Hills?

But he outlived his friends and folk

And when, years later, he awoke

He smiled his 'sleep-in-comfort' rule

There is <u>no</u> substitute for Wool.

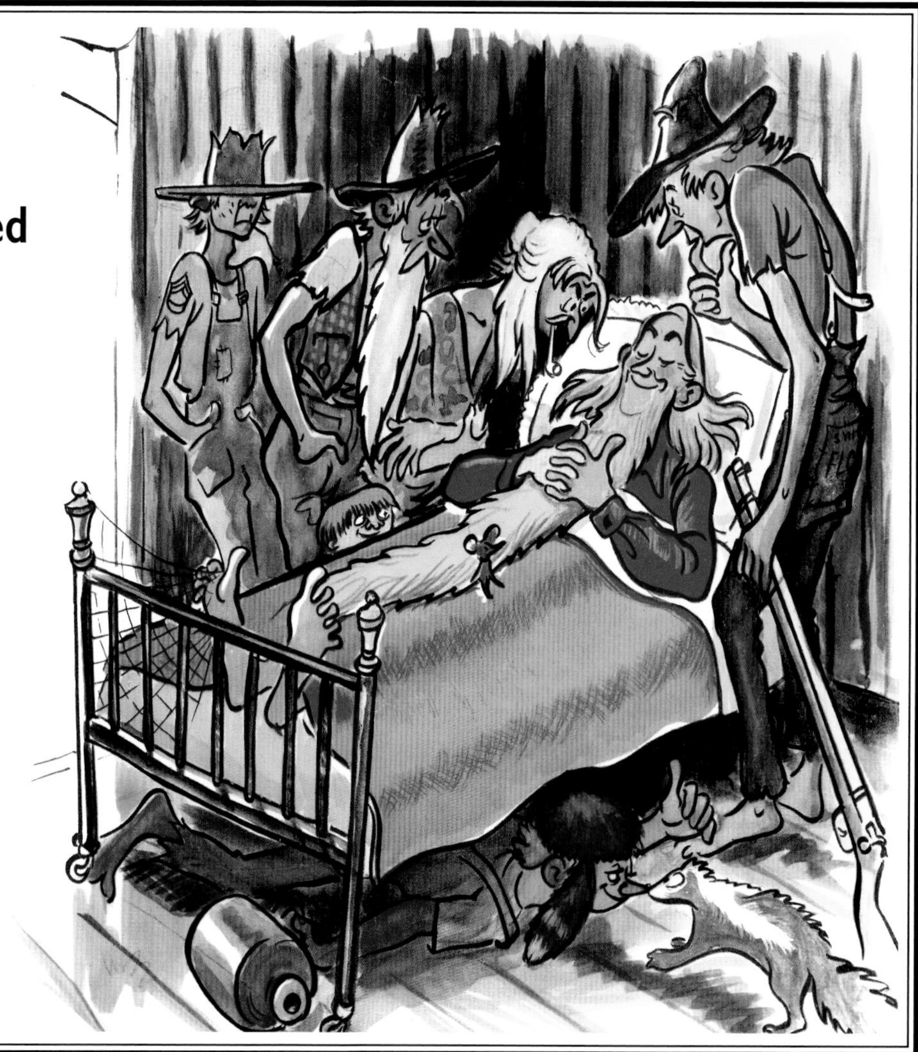

The bullies tried to roast Tom Brown.

"Confound you, put that youngster down!"

Exclaimed the Head. "The human frame

Should never be exposed to flame.

To keep out cold by day or night

Wear woollies – safe and warm and light."

And so they learned, at public school,

There is no substitute for Wool.

The badmen blanched and shook with fright
When Wyatt Earp rode into sight,
What was the secret of his power?
What made the outlaws hide and cower?
His inner glow that tamed the West
Was due to woolly shirt and vest,
So comforting where gunmen rule.
There is no substitute for Wool!
WANTED
JIM
HARDIE
DEAD
LIVE

What? Fly the Channel? Ho! ho! ho!
The sceptics jeered at Blériot.
'You'll freeze, mon ami, in that Thing -
You've nothing there but wire and string.'
But icing caused him no distress;
He flew in wool (how *did* you guess?)
The rule for all who go by plane
Is 'Rien ne remplace la laine'.*

• In any langauage, there is no substitute for wool.

Let Captain Waterhouse be praised.
Let monuments to him be raised.
You never heard of him before?
He swam to the Australian shore
(Of all the immigrants the first).
His act was bold and unrehearsed.
He took no funds, he did not pack,
But bore a sheep upon his back.
Said he: 'Tomorrow mighty flocks
Of sheep will keep the world in socks.
The generations yet to be
Will walk in comfort, thanks to me.
So do not say I look a fool,
There is no substitute for Wool.'

When Ministers begin to grouse
At awkward questions in the House
When politicians face distress
At odd disclosures in the press
We look for stuff of fitting size
For pulling o'er our master's eyes
We then recall the golden rule:
There is no substitute for Wool!

Alas, for Albert Hammel's dream!

His horseless carriage sprayed out steam.

How dankly did the moisture fall!

A soggy time was had by all.

What sneezes echoed through the land!

But those of his historic band

Who dressed in wool were never ill,

For wool absorbs but does not chill,

Which underlines the old, old rule:

There is no substitute for Wool.

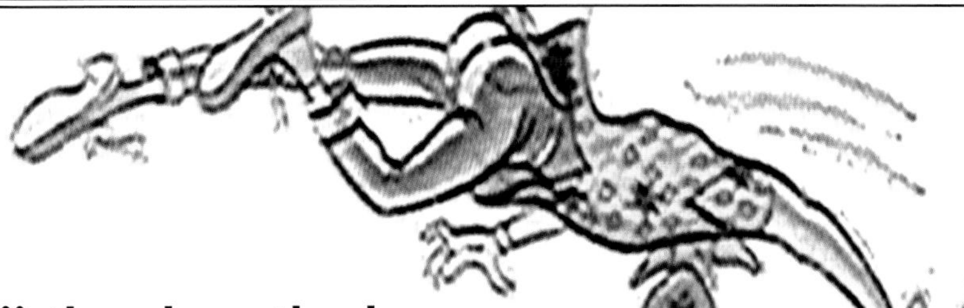

"Man, dig that crazy square," they breathed,

When May grooved in, in woollies sheathed.

"A mouldy fig, no hipster she;

A longhair of pure pedigree."

But May is gone; she hears them not

Because her jive is really hot.

She knows that when the music's cool

There is no substitute Wool!

WOOL SECRETARIAT IS INDEBTED TO MR. & MRS. J. HOROVITZ, LONDON, W.1.,
FOR SUBMITTING THE ORIGINAL RHYME UPON WHICH THIS ADVERTISEMENT IS BASED
MON REPOSE
The problem in a satellite
Is where to put the cat at night;
For if you want your mind at ease
How can you let poor Pussy freeze?
The answer reads on your computor-
"A woolly overcoat will suit her",
From sheep to Bleep all know the rule
There is no substitute for Wool.

Notes and Sources

Page 2: Acknowledgement to The Woolmark Company, successors to the International Wool Secretariat.

Page 3: Title page.

Page 4: Dedication to Peter Valpy, Past Master of the Worshipful Company of Woolmen, who died during his year of office on 16th November 1999.

Page 5: Contents.

Page 6: Photograph of H.R.H. The Princess Royal with the editor at Painters' Hall in January 1992 unveiling the painting by Michael Noakes of Her Royal Highness being admitted to the Worshipful Company of Woolmen at Cutlers' Hall on 20th October 1988. As Michael Noakes gave several sittings to each member of the Court shown in the painting it had taken four years to complete.
Guo Bing Guang took this captivating photograph to record a magical evening in the City.

Page 7: Foreword by H.R.H. The Princess Royal.

Page 9: Preface by Richard Proctor, Editor.

Page 11: Early Apeman (Pliocene) — This was the last epoch of Earth's Tertiary Period about two million years ago. Modern invertebrates and mammals were evolving at this time. This cartoon shows one of London's famous red buses as well as the Italian scooter that was all the rage in 1950s London.

Page 12: Jason — A mythological Greek hero, sent by his uncle Pelios to recover the Golden Fleece which was guarded by a dragon. He and his companions, the Argonauts, returned with the Fleece after many adventures.

Page 13: Jupiter — The principal Roman god equivalent to the Greek god, Zeus. The home of the gods in ancient times was said to be Mount Olympus but here the cartoonist intentionally confuses it with the London Underground station Olympia just as he introduces a bottle of beer as nectar, the drink of the gods.

Page 14: Helen — In Greek legend she was the very beautiful daughter of the god Zeus and Leda, who married Menelaus, King of Sparta and then ran away to Troy with Paris. Thus started the Trojan War recorded by Homer in the Iliad. According to the poet Marlowe, Helen had "the face that launched a thousand ships".

Page 15: Venus — Roman goddess identified with Aphrodite, the Greek goddess of love. She is perhaps best known today by her portrayal arising naked from the sea in the painting by Renaissance painter Botticelli.

Page 16: Jonah — An Old Testament figure, who tried to escape God's orders and was thrown into the sea where he was swallowed by "a great fish". In the Bible description he was not nearly as happy inside the fish as this cartoon suggests.

Page 17: King Midas — A legendary Greek King who wished that everything he touched be turned to gold. When his wish was granted he found it very inconvenient as he could neither eat nor drink. Luckily for him he was released from this unfortunate fate.

Page 18: Socrates — An Athenian philosopher (469-399 B.C.). His method of teaching was by asking questions to expose the inadequacy of others' thought. This was the beginning of "logic". His stand against tyranny whether by oligarchs or the mob made him unpopular and he was condemned to death by drinking hemlock.

Page 19: Pythagoras — A Greek philosopher of the 6th century B.C. who founded a religious society at Crotone in Southern Italy, whose members followed strict dietary rules and interpreted the physical world through numbers. He probably discovered the geometrical theorem which bears his name, namely that the square on the hypotenuse in a right-angled triangle is equal to the sum of the squares of the other two sides.

Page 20: Nero, Roman Emperor (37-68 A.D.) — Notorious for his cruelty, he was much hated in Rome and popularly supposed to have played a musical instrument while the city was on fire. The Latin "Quo vadis?" might be translated as "Where are you going?" or a sentry's cry "Who goes there?"

Page 21: Cleopatra (69-30 B.C.) — She was the mistress of two Roman emperors, Julius Caesar and later Mark Anthony. Until 48 B.C. she was joint ruler of Egypt with her brother, Ptolemy XIII, but in this year he deposed her. She is said to have had herself delivered into Caesar's presence in a roll of carpet after which he restored her to the throne. Shakespeare following Plutarch's account uses her life story for his great play Anthony and Cleopatra.

Page 22: Ancient Britons — Hengist and Horsa were legendary leaders of the first Anglo-Saxon settlers in Britain. The Anglo-Saxon Chronicle, which was not written until the late 9th century, claimed that Horsa was killed in 455 A.D. and that Hengist ruled Kent from 455 to 488 A.D.

Page 23: Santa Claus — A legendary figure probably based on St Nicholas, the 4th century patron saint of Russia, sailors and children, whose relics are in the Basilica of S.Nicola at Bari. The story of his gift of gold to three poor girls led to the habit of exchanging gifts on his feast day, the 6th of December. This now happens in most countries on the 25th of December. Santa Claus or Father Christmas is usually depicted with a long white beard and a red coat, driving through the snow in a sleigh filled with presents. Yule is an archaic word for the Christmas Festival but is not a perfect rhyme for wool.

Page 24: Wenceslas — 10th century Duke of Bohemia (924-929 A.D.), who brought Christianity to a pagan country. A conspiracy among the nobles led to his murder by his own brother. He is now patron saint of the Czech Republic.

Page 25: King Arthur — From medieval times a vast number of stories have been told about this legendary King of Britain and his knights. Most record the lady Guinevere as his not always faithful Queen and tell of a round table where all knights were equal.

Page 26: Lady Godiva — The English wife of Leofric, the 11th century Earl of Mercia. According to the 13th century chronicler Roger of Wendover she rode naked through the market place of Coventry in order to persuade her husband to reduce the taxes he had imposed on the town.

Page 27: Macbeth, King of the Scots (1040-1057) — After killing Duncan, he usurped the throne and ruled until defeated by Duncan's son, Malcolm. However he is best remembered as the eponymous hero of Shakespeare's tragedy and it is in Act IV of this play that we find the well known reference to witches and strange ingredients in their cauldron. What Scots wear under their kilts is a question often asked by the English but seldom answered by a Scot.

Page 28: Robin Hood — An English outlaw, probably legendary, who was the hero of ballads dating from the 14th century. He was famous for his skill with the longbow and for killing the evil Sheriff of Nottingham.

Page 29: King John — He was King of England from 1199 to 1216. His reign was notable for conflict with the Papacy and his own barons. In 1216 John prepared to march on London but, while crossing the Wash, lost all his treasure and baggage. He returned to Swinestead Abbey where he died.

Page 30: William Tell — A Swiss national hero first mentioned in a 15th century story, who fought for Swiss independence from the Austrian Hapsburg Empire. In Schiller's play of 1804, after refusing to do homage as required by Gessler, the Austrian governor, he was ordered to shoot an apple from his son's head with a crossbow at 80 paces. He succeeded without harming his son and sometime later had the satisfaction of killing Gessler.

Page 31: Henry V (1387-1422) — As King of England he defeated the French decisively at Agincourt. The longbow was at this time the most effective weapon of war and particularly so against the heavily armoured French knights, who had difficulty getting up again when knocked off their horses. The battle is especially well known as it is a central scene in Shakespeare's play Henry V.

Page 32: Gutenberg — Johann Gutenberg (c.1400-c.1468) after many years of development work invented a method of printing with movable type. In 1455 he printed the famous Gutenberg Bible. In 1950s England men were most anxious to have " knife edge" creases in their trousers and a great deal of research led to a process which achieved this in wool cloth.

Page 33: King Philip / Jan van Eyck — Before 1430 the great painter Jan van Eyck went on two missions to Iberia to paint portraits of prospective brides. A little poetic licence here, as these trips were not for King Philip of Spain, who was not born until 1478, but for Philip, Duke of Burgundy, van Eyck's patron. The second journey was a success. Van Eyck's portrait of the Infanta of Portugal, Isabella, pleased the duke and the embassy returned with her to Bruges for a wedding held on 7th January 1430.

Page 34: Christopher Columbus (1451-1506) — An Italian navigator who discovered America. He was hoping to reach the East by sailing westward round the world. A retired pirate he obtained the backing of Ferdinand and Isabella, the Spanish monarchs, and set sail on the 3rd of August 1492 reaching the Bahamas on the 12th of October. The members of his crew were largely drawn from the uneducated undesirables of the port of Palos and terrified they might fall off the edge of a flat world.

Page 35: Leonardo da Vinci (1452-1519) — He was an Italian artist and scientific genius. In addition to painting some of the greatest pictures of all time such as the fresco of the Last Supper in Milan and the Mona Lisa in the Louvre, he became a military engineer to Cesare Borgia and left notebooks which show his wide range of interests including anatomy, botany, geology and mechanics.

Page 36: Anne Boleyn (c.1507-1536) — She was the second wife of Henry VIII, the King of England, who married six times. She was mother of Queen Elizabeth I of England but Henry soon tired of her. She was accused of treason by committing adultery, taken to the Tower of London and executed.

Page 37: Anne of Cleves — Henry VIII took her as his fourth wife on the advice of his minister Cromwell, who wished to strengthen the Protestant cause in England by an alliance with Germany. Known as his Flanders Mare she was not at all pretty — Henry divorced her and had Cromwell condemned for treason and executed.

Page 38: William Shakespeare (1564-1616) — The dramatist and poet who is accepted as England's greatest writer. He was born in Stratford-upon-Avon and married Anne Hathaway in 1582. Soon afterwards he went to London and became an actor. Written after 1589 his first plays were historical. These were followed by his early comedies, Love's Labours Lost, The Two Gentlemen of Verona and The Taming of the Shrew. After these, from 1595 to 1600, came A Midsummer Night's Dream, Much Ado About Nothing, Twelfth Night and As You Like It. Later he wrote the major tragedies, Hamlet, Othello, King Lear and Macbeth, and finally the more experimental plays including A Winter's Tale and The Tempest. In 1611 he returned to Stratford, dying in 1616. After his death 36 plays were collected in 1623 and published in what is known as The First Folio. In addition to these great plays his poetry included Venus and Adonis and The Rape of Lucrece as well as his Sonnets.

Page 39: Samuel Pepys (1633-1703) — Most famous for the diary, which he kept from 1660-1669. A wonderful book in its own right and also a valuable historical source as it covers the period from the restoration of Charles II through the Plague and Great Fire of London. His career in naval administration culminated in his appointment as secretary to the Admiralty. In addition he was a Member of Parliament, President of the Royal Society and Master of the Worshipful Company of Clothworkers. Pudding Lane where the Great Fire started can still be found off Eastcheap in the City. The diary was written in a method of shorthand popular in the 17th century and based on Shelton's system which had already run to three editions before Pepys went to Cambridge in 1650. Your editor cannot interpret the squiggles in this verse and fears that they are decorative rather than shorthand for "There is no substitute for Wool".

Page 40: Benjamin Franklin (1706-1790) — He was an American diplomat, a scientist and writer. Although perhaps most famous as a diplomat around the time of the American Revolution and for his help in drafting the American Declaration of Independence he experimented with static electricity and even invented the lightning conductor after a dangerous attempt to fly a kite in a storm.

Page 41: Judge Jeffreys (c.1645-1689) — He was a supporter of King James II, King of England, and became Lord Chancellor. After the Monmouth rebellion he imposed harsh punishments and many death sentences at what became known as the Bloody Assizes held in Dorchester. Following the downfall of James II he was imprisoned and executed. It is a particularly nice idea in this verse that if he had worn wool he would have put the prisoners on probation — a lenient non-custodial sentence.

Page 42: Louis XV, King of France (1715-1774) — His indecisiveness during his reign contributed to the outbreak of the French Revolution in 1789. He was much influenced by his mistresses especially Madame de Pompadour and later Madame du Barry. His reign was best summed up by Madame de Pompadour when she said "Apres nous le deluge" or "After us the deluge".

Page 43: Samuel Johnson (1709-1784) — An important and great English writer, who published his dictionary in 1755. The house where it was compiled over a seven-year period can still be visited in Gough Square, off Fleet Street in London. A friend of Reynolds, Goldsmith and Burke and a great conversationalist it is still possible to enjoy his talk by reading Boswell's Life of Johnson, which was published in 1791.

Page 44: Captain Bligh (1754-1817) — A British admiral who was sent to Tahiti to collect specimens of the breadfruit tree. On the return voyage the crew of his ship, the Bounty, mutinied and cast him adrift in a small boat with 18 officers and no chart. He survived to be appointed governor of New South Wales in 1805 but again he quarrelled with his subordinates and returned to England in 1811.

Page 45: Giovanni Casanova (1725-1798) — An Italian adventurer famous for his romantic liaisons. His memoirs record his love affairs and his adventures, the most famous of which was his escape from the prison in Venice in 1756. Mr John Fitzgerald the author of this verse is to be congratulated on his punning use of "Venetian blinds".

Page 46: Ballet originated in the formal dances of the French court entertainments under Louis XIV. In the18th century it became established in the public theatres but this cartoon has typical 1950s associations with a hotwater bottle and a man wearing a cap in the background.

Page 47: Lord Horatio Nelson (1758-1805) — The most famous English admiral and as Thomas Carlyle has told us he was a hero. Quite young he lost the sight in his right eye at Calvi but later put this loss to good use at the battle of Cape St Vincent when he refused to recognise the signal to retreat by putting his telescope to his blind eye. In 1798 he destroyed French naval power in the Mediterranean at the Battle of the Nile when he lost his right arm in action. Returning to a hero's welcome he caused considerable scandal by his affair with Lady Hamilton. In 1805 the French fleet escaped from blockaded Toulon with Nelson in pursuit. At the Battle of Trafalgar Nelson won a great victory but was mortally wounded. His last words to the captain of his flag ship, the Victory, are said to have been "Kiss me Hardy" or possibly "Kismet, Hardy". Nelson is buried at St Paul's cathedral and commemorated at Guildhall in the City. By public subscription the famous Nelson's column was erected between 1839 and 1842 in Trafalgar Square. It should be noted that 2005 is the bicentenary of his death.

Page 48: George Brummell (1778-1840) — Known as Beau Brummell he was a prominent English dandy taking enormous care of his appearance. He was a close friend of the Prince Regent, who later became George IV of England. In 1816 he fled to France to evade his creditors. There he lived a sad life seldom visited by his English friends and died in an asylum.

Page 49: George Stephenson (1781-1848) — He was a British engineer, who built his first locomotive in 1815. After a number of improved models he produced the Rocket in 1829. It carried passengers at 36 miles per hour (58 kph) and its success encouraged railway development in Europe and North America.

Page 50: Highland Crofters — Crofting was a system of farming in the Highlands of Scotland, where families cultivated a small area of land and had access to common grazing land. The introduction of sheep in the late 18th century destroyed much of the system but led to a home weaving industry. Sassenach is a Gaelic word used in Scotland for an Englishman. It is, of course, slightly derogatory.

Page 51: Rip Van Winkle — He was a character in a short story by Washington Irving, 1783-1859. Published in his collection of 1819-1820 "The Sketch Book" it tells the story of a man who falls asleep for 20 years and wakes to find he has slept through the American War of Independence. The Catskill Mountains are a range in the United States of America not far from New York and part of the North Appalachian Mountains.

Page 52: Tom Brown — First published in 1857 Tom Brown's School Days tells the story of a boy at Rugby School under the headmastership of Dr Arnold. Rugby was a Victorian public school, called public because any parent who could pay the fees could enter his son. At this time Dr Arnold and other headmasters like Thring at Uppingham were trying to instil high moral standards in their pupils. The book's most dramatic and best known scene occurs towards the middle when Tom is bullied by the villain, Flashman, who roasts him in front of an open fire. The anonymous author who had been at the school was particularly keen to draw attention to bullying as a morally reprehensible practice.

Page 53: Wyatt Earp (1849-1929) — With his two brothers Wyatt Earp kept the peace in the cattle capitals of Kansas, where he caused no great trouble. Later when the group moved to Arizona they took part in the famous gunfight at O.K. Corral in Tombstone, Arizona. This is thought to have been a fight between sheepmen and cowmen set off by alcohol. The three Earps and Doc Holliday faced Ike Clanton's gang. Within 60 seconds, three of Clanton's associates were dead and both Earp brothers wounded. It is uncertain who was in the right but Tombstone is said to have become a safer place. Earp survived several more gunfights and moved to California, dying on 13th January 1929 in Los Angeles.

Page 54: Louis Blériot (1872-1936) — A French aviator who was the first to fly over the English Channel from Calais to Dover in 1909. Appropriately the French " Rien ne replace la laine" replaces the usual last line.

Page 55: Captain Waterhouse — Well may the author of this rhyme write: "You never heard of him?" Your editor struggled to find a reference to him and is indebted to "Pioneers of Wool" published in 1972 by Richard Ingpen for the following historical information. Apparently between 1461 and 1483 sheep were sent from Northleach in England to supplement the Royal Flock of the King of Spain and much later in 1796 Captain Waterhouse brought 13 Merinos of Spanish decent to Australia. These sheep are said to be the progenitors of the Australian Wool Industry.

Page 56: Questions in the House — The "House" is the House of Commons at the Palace of Westminster where Members of Parliament can within certain rules question ministers and even the Prime Minister. The answers are prepared by civil servants to help their ministers tell the truth or as much of the truth as seems wise. The rhyme confirms that "leaks and spin" were already well understood in the 1950s.

Page 57: Albert Hammel — was a Danish industrialist who commissioned Hans Ulrich Johansen to build a car in 1886. It was brought to England in 1954 and run in the London to Brighton Rally. The oldest automobile which can still be operated, it is on display in Helsinore, Denmark. For this information your editor is indebted to Joe Saward who answered my cry for knowledge placed in the Question Book at the Athenaeum, London.

Page 58: "When May grooved in..." — is a rhyme which makes use of the dance slang of the 1950s. Jive is the name of the jazz dancing of the period. "Grooved" and "hipster" are not too obscure to guess but "mouldy fig " is more difficult. Spelt "moldy fig" without a "u" it can be found in American dictionaries of slang defined as an old fashion person or a "square".

Page 59: The Trouble with a Satellite — This takes us back to the time of the very first journeys into space. The rhyme was written by Mr Horovitz, still a resident of Notting Hill, a part of London made famous by a recent film. The original poster hangs in his hall and, as it was the only known copy, his wife and I took it to a photographer who reproduced it for publication in this collection. It is interesting to note that 'computer' is spelt with an 'o', because in those earlier times a computer was a human calculater.

The Worshipful Company of Woolmen — A short historical note.

The City of London Livery Companies began in medieval times as guilds to protect the interests of particular trades and their practitioners. The first recorded reference to the Woolmen's Company was in 1180 during the reign of King Henry II when, with 19 other guilds, it was fined for functioning without a licence.

In 1336 King Edward III negotiated a specific tax on wool and arranged for "The English Wool Company" to finance his war with France, which was later called "the Hundred Years War".

King Henry VIII granted incorporation of the Company in 1522 and finally on 29th March 1825 the Company was granted livery by the Court of Aldermen of the City of London.

For hundreds of years when wool prospered so did the nation.

So concerned was Queen Elizabeth I about the wool trade that she had Parliament make everyone over the age of six (except the wealthiest) wear on Sundays "a cap of wool knit and dressed in England". Under Charles II Parliament passed a law requiring coffins to be lined in fleece and shrouds to be made of wool.

In 1988 HRH The Princess Royal became the first Lady Liveryman of the Company and in the same year Lord Mackay of Clashfern, The Lord Chancellor of the United Kingdom and Northern Ireland, who sits on the Woolsack in the House of Lords, became a Freeman Honoris Causa of the Company.

Hundreds of years ago a wealthy wool merchant had the following engraved on the windows of his house. "I praise God and ever shall – it is the sheep had paid for all". Today we say "There is no substitute for wool".

The Writers

The authors of these rhymes come in two categories. There were the amateurs who responded to the challenge of a public competition rather than the five pound cash prize. Amongst these we have already mentioned Mr Horovitz, who wrote the" Satellite". In addition some received their five pounds but found the rhyme was never used. This was the case with "Socrates" a very clever rhyme by Mr P.N.G. Gilbert, who by coincidence went on to be Master of the Woolmen's Company in 1985. But there was another category of writer brought in by the success of the campaign. They were professional writers at the top of their profession like E.S. Turner who wrote for Punch, the most famous magazine in England. Now in his 90s, he is still writing wittily for magazines.

The International Wool Secretariat was indebted to the following successful competitors:
Miss E M Blake of Hampstead for "Jupiter" on page 13.
Mr Charles Panshon of Levenshulme, Manchester for "Venus" on page 15.
Miss Nadine Peppard of London for "Jonah" on page 16.
Mr Philip Kelleway of Great Missenden for "King Midas" on page 17.
Miss Julia Fuller of Hornsey for "Cleopatra" on page 21.
Mrs H Farmer of Putney for "King John" on page 29.
Mr David Livingstone of London for "William Tell" on page 30.
Mr P G S Muttlebury of Warwick Wold, Surrey for "Henry V" on page 31.
Miss D Tindall of London for "Dr Johnson" on page 43.
Mr John Fitzgerald of London for "Casanova" on page 45.
Miss A Hutchings of London for "Ballerina" on page 46.
Mr L Fitzmaurice of London for "Rip Van Winkle" on page 51.
Mr A F Duke of Twickenham for "Tom Brown" on page 52.

The Cartoonists

The illustrators of the rhymes were both established cartoonists and illustrators working in the field of advertising. The public at the time were familiar with many of the names, such as Hewison, Petty and Mahood, whose cartoons would appear regularly in the famous weekly magazine Punch, first published in July 1841 and which only ceased publication in June 2002, but was at the height of its popularity in the 1950s. Many of the illustrations were done by Mr Derek Waller who worked for the International Wool Secretariat and was keenly involved in the production of the campaign. The editor is grateful for his assistance in compiling this edition. The observant reader will find that we are able to acknowledge the following cartoonists:

Page 19 Pythagoras by Petty. Page 23 Santa Claus by Hewison.
Page 25 King Arthur by Derek Waller
Page 27 Macbeth by Derek Waller. Page 33 King Philip by Cockerill. Page 34 Columbus by Petty.
Page 35 Leonardo by Hewison. Page 37 Anne of Cleves by Derek Waller.
Page 40 Benjamin Franklin by Mahood.
Page 41 Judge Jeffreys by Derek Waller. Page 47 Lord Nelson by Derek Waller.
Page 48 Beau Brummell by Derek Waller. Page 49 George Stephenson by Mahood.
Page 54 Louis Bleriot by Cockerill. Page 55 Captain Waterhouse by Peter Probyn.
Page 57 Albert Hammel by Tilley.